DuelMasters

For most people, Duel Masters is just a fun game, but for some it is much more. A few special players can actually bring the card creatures to life! These players are masters, and they need passion and discipline, as well as a type of martial art called Kaijudo, "The Art of Battling with Giant Monsters". A true Duel Master knows exactly which card to play at exactly the right moment. They make decisions in less than a split second!

SHOBU
KIRIFUDA

Shobu Kirifuda loves playing Duel Masters and he is a passionate duellist, but he has not yet learned his true potential. He finds that he can tap into the power of another dimension, where the creatures and the magic of the game really exist!

Shobu's father was a powerful Kaijudo master, but he vanished years ago into the card dimension. Shobu has the same power and, in search of his father, he is always gaining skill as a duellist. What seems to be an ordinary game is a very real battle for Shobu!

DuelMasters

Licensing by:

Hasbro
Properties
Group

Pedigree®

OFFICIAL
Wizards
OF THE COAST
LICENSED PRODUCT

Published by Pedigree Books Limited
Beech Hill House, Walnut Gardens, Exeter, Devon EX4 4DH.
E-mail books@pedigreegroup.co.uk
Published 2004

£6.99

F I R E

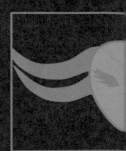

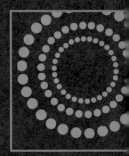

CIVILIZATION

During an Ancient War between Dragonoids and Humans, a powerful weapon made most of the mountains become active volcanoes and the Fire civilisation suffered terrible volcanic activities.

The islands of the Fire civilisation are covered in volcanic ash and hardened magma. There are constant earthquakes and volcanic eruptions and the climate is very dry and hot.

Fire creatures use mining to get iron, gunpowder, magma and

steam. Once a mountain has been mined, they turn it into a fortress. They build steam engines for transportation and mining, and use the clouds of smoke and steam to hide them from their enemies. Dragonoids have learned how to force a volcano eruption and use it as a weapon. This 'volcano weapon' is totally destructive.

Fire creatures are very confident and aggressive, They seek total victory over their enemies and show no mercy. Even when losing, they refuse to surrender. They fight to the death proudly!

LIGHTS

CIVILIZATION

The Lights world is a rich and advanced civilisation. They have lots of resources and powerful technology, so other civilisations are always trying to invade and steal from them. The Lights civilisation has to be aggressive and fight to keep their world safe from invaders.

Lights creatures believe in order and obedience. Compared to the other civilisations, the population in the Lights world is small, but each individual is very powerful. Lots of Lights creatures have shiny bodies and hover in the air with their weapons close by.

Lights inhabitants live in mid-air above the clouds, on floating islands. They are not affected by gravity. The main city is surrounded by lots of small colonies, and all the buildings are made of alloys and energy fields.

NATURE

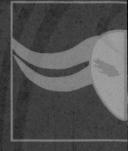

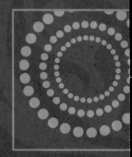

CIVILIZATION

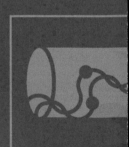

The Nature civilisation is based on the largest continent, covered by an enormous jungle. It is hot and humid, but very little sunlight gets through the tall trees above. There are lots of races in the Nature world, but there are no cities and no one race is in charge – whoever has the most power wins. Strength matters more than technology. Even Beast Folk, the most intelligent of the races, only have basic technology.

The trees on the Nature world store energy. They are so tall they almost touch the cities in the Lights world! There is too much gravity on this world, so creatures from other civilisations find it hard to move in the heavy atmosphere. Nature creatures are amazingly strong! Some races tattoo their bodies with special designs and symbols.

The Darkness and Water civilisations are a serious threat to the Nature lifestyle. They have to go to war to fight for survival!

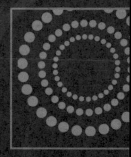
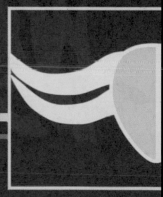

DARKNESS

CIVILIZATION

The Darkness civilisation is a huge underground world, full of fearsome creatures! The air is filled with toxic gas and there is no light. The inhabitants are always looking for the secret of immortality, so they can live forever. But their experiments have made deadly diseases, confused the space-time continuum and spoiled the world around them. It is a dangerous and poisonous place!

Darkness creatures wear masks and armour made of bone. Their flesh is rotting off from the toxic gas and diseases that fill their world. After living in darkness for so long, most Darkness creatures are completely blind.

To survive the toxic gas, Darkness creatures keep their masks on at all times. Even outside the dark world, they can't survive without gas masks.

Darkness inhabitants think of nothing but their search for immortality. Driven by madness and selfishness, tortured by fear and despair, their lives are a struggle to conquer and control!

WATER

CIVILIZATION

The world of Water is half-land, half-sea. Inhabitants can live in both environments. They prefer learning and research to real action. In war they depend on strategies and tactics rather than direct attack. They are controlled by Cyber Lords, and many Water creatures have a chip installed in their bodies. They communicate and exchange information telepathically.

The secret source of energy for this civilisation is in a hidden ocean current. Only a few very powerful creatures know this important secret.

Cities are built deep in the ocean because it has more energy resources. At the centre is the Tower, shaped like a spiral, where the Cyber Lords float in their cylinders. All around the Tower are transparent buildings, made from hardened seawater.

Some Water creatures can change their body shape to fit the environment. They can also control the seawater around them, converting it into a weapon, armour, clothing or transportation for land or sea.

THE REAL DEAL

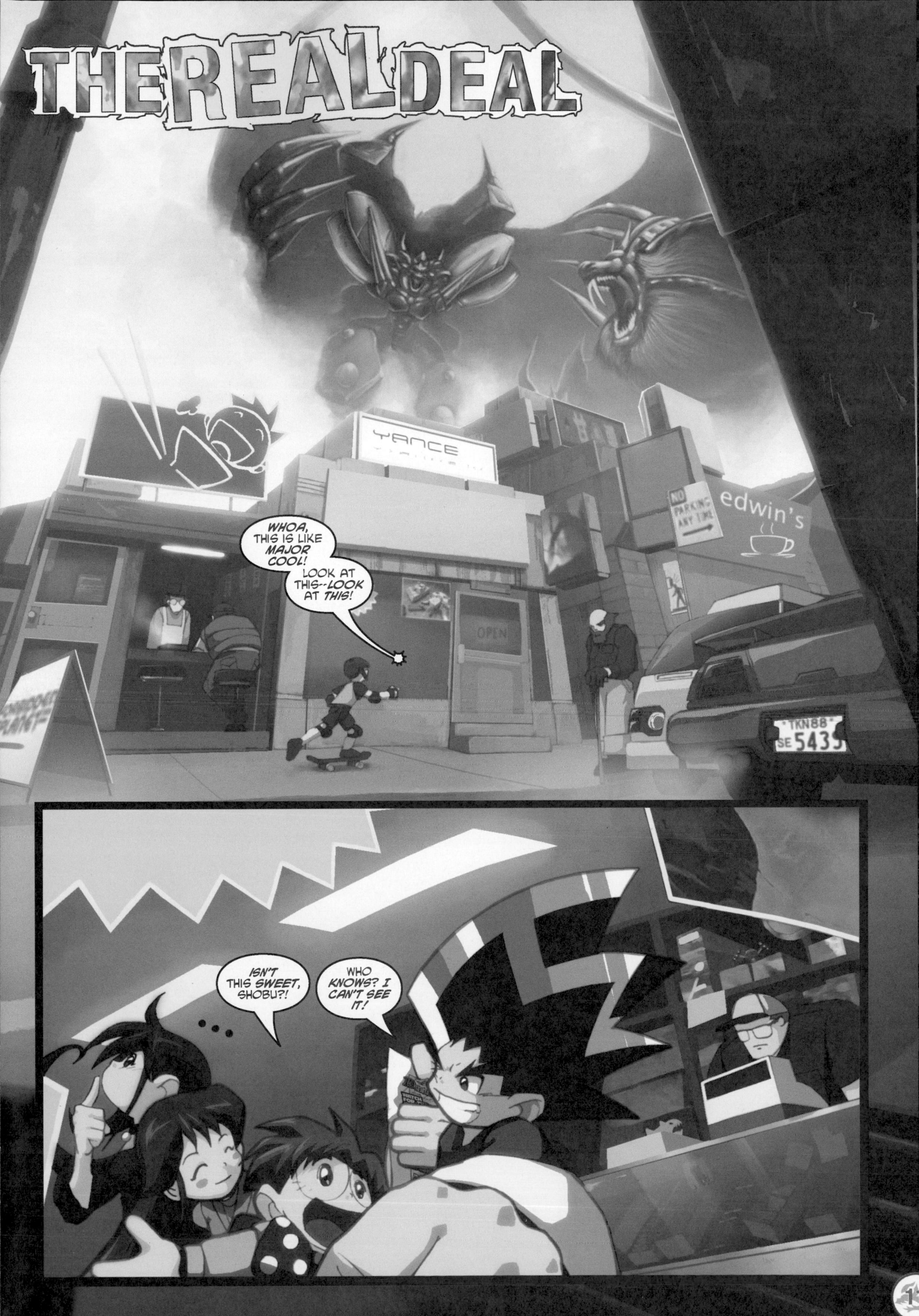

HOW AM I SUPPOSED TO READ *ANYTHING* WITH YOU SHOVING IT *THROUGH* MY HEAD!

CAN YOU READ IT *NOW*, YOUR HIGHNESS?

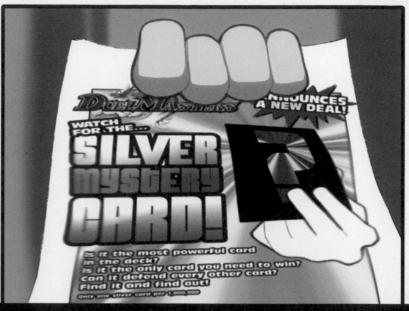

DUEL MASTERS ANNOUNCES A NEW DEAL!

WATCH FOR THE...
SILVER MYSTERY CARD!

Is it the most powerful card in the deck?
Is it the only card you need to win?
Can it defend every other card?
Find it and find out!

Only one silver card per 1,000,000

IF A DUELIST HAD *THAT* CARD THEY'D BE *UNBEATABLE!*

EVEN REKUTA MIGHT FINALLY BE ABLE TO WIN.

THIS IS *SO-O-O COOL* I'M GOING TO PRETEND I DIDN'T HEAR THAT, MIMI.

SO, YOU DON'T CARE--?

I DON'T WANT TO OVER DO IT. IT WASN'T THAT LONG AGO THAT I THOUGHT *I* COULDN'T LOSE.

IT'S NOT THAT, SAYUKI--SINCE THAT DAY I'VE BEGUN TO SEE THE GAME IN A *NEW WAY...*

THIS IS ABOUT LOSING TO *KNIGHT?* BUT HE'S A *REAL MASTER!*

I HEAR YOU'RE REALLY GOOD AT SWIFT ATTACKS. WHY DON'T YOU LEAD OFF.

OKAY, *NOW* YOU'RE GONNA SEE MY *BEST* GAME! I'M HOLDING NOTHING BACK!

HOW ABOUT *THAT* MOVE?!

IF THAT'S YOUR BEST, WE'VE GOT A *LONG* WAY TO GO.

LET ME SHOW YOU WHAT A REAL DUEL MASTER WOULD DO.

YOU HAVE TO LEARN TO CONCENTRATE.

WHAT--?!

WHEN YOU CONCENTRATE *MANA* IS GENERATED.

MANA GIVE YOUR POWER TO *THIS* CARD...

I SUMMON THE *DEADLY FIGHTER BRAID CLAW!*

CONCENTRATE BEFORE YOU MAKE YOUR NEXT MOVE.

OKAY. MANA IS *GENERATED.*

I SUMMON THE *FATAL ATTACKER HORVATH!*

HOW'S THAT--?

GOOD BUT NOT GOOD ENOUGH. DON'T TRY TO *BEAT* ME, TRY TO *WIN.*

NOW I SUMMON *CRIMSON HAMMER!*

NO--THAT WILL DESTROY MY ATTACKER HORVATH!

NOW I WILL ATTACK YOUR SHIELDS WITH BRAID CLAW!

WHOA!

I CAN'T WATCH!

SWIFT ATTACKS WORK IN TOURNAMENTS, SHOBU, BUT NOT ALWAYS IN *LIFE*.

IF YOU'RE GOING TO BE A TRUE DUEL MASTER, YOU ARE GOING TO HAVE TO UNDERSTAND YOUR *POWER*...

...YOU CAN'T JUST PLAY FROM YOUR HEAD. YOU HAVE TO PLAY FROM YOUR *HEART* AS WELL.

YOU DON'T HAVE TO *BEAT* ME TO WIN.

I'LL DO *BOTH!*

SHOBU HAS ONLY ONE SHIELD CARD LEFT! HE'S *DOOMED!*

SORRY KID, I THOUGHT YOU HAD IT. BUT I'VE BEEN WRONG BEFORE.

DO YOU WANT TO FINISH, OR DO YOU WANT TO LEAVE?

I ONLY HAVE ONE SHIELD CARD LEFT. I DON'T HAVE ENOUGH CARDS...

...I CAN'T POSSIBLY *WIN!*

16

IT'S OKAY, YOU PLAYED WELL!

YEAH, YOU REALLY OWNED THE ZONE!

I DIDN'T OWN *ANYTHING*.

NOW YOU'RE SOUNDING LIKE A DUEL MASTER. BUT *SOUNDING* LIKE ONE AND *BEING* ONE ARE TWO DIFFERENT THINGS.

IF YOU CONTINUE TO PLAY, I'M PROBABLY GOING TO WIN.

BUT I CAN BEAT YOU, AND YOU CAN *STILL* WIN. *THAT'S* WHAT "OWNING THE ZONE" IS.

REC

SAT 00: 34: 15

BUT IF YOU CAN'T UNDERSTAND THIS THEN YOU CAN'T BE A DUEL MASTER AND YOU MIGHT AS WELL *QUIT*.

THEN...

...I QUIT.

BECAUSE I CAN'T BEAT HIM. I'M GONNA LOSE.

NO SHOBU! WHY?!

SHOBU, YOU LIKE PLAYING WITH THE CARDS DON'T YOU?

YEAH! IT'S FUN!

BUT SOMETIMES YOU MAY BE BEATEN.

BUT YOU *SHOULD* STILL PLAY.

REMEMBER TO ALWAYS DO YOUR *BEST*, THEN YOU WILL ALWAYS WIN.

OKAY, DAD!

PROMISE?

I *PROMISE*!

TRUST IN YOURSELF AND *NEVER* GIVE UP.

WAIT, I JUST REMEMBERED A PROMISE I MADE A LONG TIME AGO. I'M *NOT* QUITTING!

IF I DO MY BEST AND NEVER GIVE UP, I'LL ALWAYS WIN!

OKAY, MR. KNIGHT, LET'S *FINISH* THIS!

I RESPECT THAT. BUT, HOW ARE YOU GOING TO FIGHT BACK?

YOU HAVE ONLY ONE SHIELD LEFT...!

A DUEL IS LIKE LIFE-- YOU NEVER KNOW WHAT'S GOING TO HAPPEN.

I SUMMON THE *BOLSHACK DRAGON!*

YOU PLAYED WELL, KID, BUT THIS IS THE END...

I SUMMON THE *HOLY AWE.*

THE WORLD AS WE KNOW IT, IS NOT THE WORLD AROUND US. THERE'S *MUCH* MORE THAN MOST PEOPLE EVER REALIZE.

WHOA...

THERE IS ANOTHER REALM... A *WORLD* LIKE OURS IN SOME WAYS.

BUT *VASTLY* DIFFERENT IN MANY OTHERS.

IT'S A WORLD OF ONGOING UPHEAVAL AND CONFLAGRATION.

A WORLD CONSTANTLY AT *WAR!*

IT IS FROM THIS REALM THAT THE CREATURES OF DUEL MASTERS COME. THE GAME IS A *BRIDGE* BETWEEN WORLDS.

YOU MEAN THE MONSTERS ARE *REAL!*

YES. THROUGH SOME MYSTICAL MEANS, THE CREATURES ARE SUMMONED TO AN EXTRA-DIMENSIONAL BATTLE ZONE WHEN SUMMONED IN THE GAME.

THEY REALLY FIGHT THE BATTLES OUR CARDS CHOREOGRAPH.

AND WE NEVER EVEN SUSPECT IT!

WELL...A TRUE MASTER CAN "SEE" THE CREATURES DURING THE GAME.

HAVE YOU HAD... FLASHES OF SIGHT-- PERHAPS *IMAGES* IN YOUR MIND WHEN YOU DUEL?

YES...! ALMOST LIKE FLICKERING PICTURES IN THE AIR! I THOUGHT I WAS GOING NUTS.

THE MORE YOU LEARN, THE MORE YOU'LL BE ABLE TO SEE. A DUEL MASTER IS PERFECTLY ATTUNED TO THE OTHER REALM.

BUT *YOU'VE* GOT A WAYS TO GO YET.

NICE CARROT YOU'RE DANGLING THERE, MR. KNIGHT.

CAN YOU *GO* TO THIS OTHER PLACE? PHYSICALLY?

I DON'T KNOW. THERE ARE RUMORS OF THOSE WHO HAVE *TRIED*...

"...I DON'T KNOW IF ANYONE COULD SURVIVE THAT FORBIDDING PLACE..."

"...I DON'T KNOW IF ANYONE COULD SURVIVE THAT FORBIDDING PLACE..."

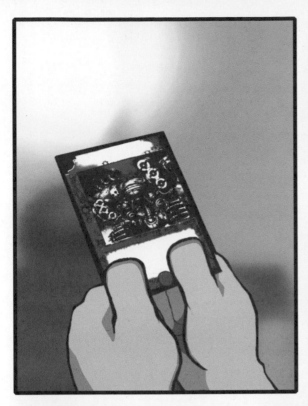

SHOBU, HONEY-- IT'S TIME FOR BED, SWEETHEART.

OKAY, MOM...

...I HAVE A *LOT* TO SLEEP ON.

GOODNIGHT MOM.

AH, THERE YOU ARE.

HOW DOES THE BOY PROGRESS?

HIS TRAINING PROGRESSES SMOOTHLY. HE'S DOING WELL.

HE'S BEEN ASKING QUESTIONS ABOUT THE *OTHER REALM*.

HE'S ALSO ASKING ABOUT HIS FATHER. I WISH I HAD SOMETHING TO TELL HIM.

THAT IS NOT A PROBLEM. PERHAPS HIS CURIOSITY WILL SPUR HIS *PROGRESS*.

PERHAPS HE WILL SOLVE A MYSTERY THAT HAS BAFFLED MANY.

KEEP AN EYE ON THE BOY. MANY ARE THEY WHO WOULD EXPLOIT HIS POWER.

I WILL BE VIGILANT. SHOBU KIRIFUDA *MUST* BE KEPT SAFE.

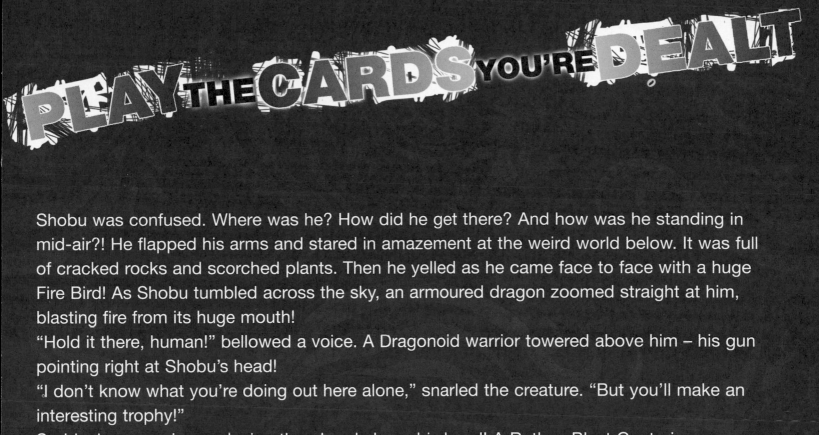

Shobu was confused. Where was he? How did he get there? And how was he standing in mid-air?! He flapped his arms and stared in amazement at the weird world below. It was full of cracked rocks and scorched plants. Then he yelled as he came face to face with a huge Fire Bird! As Shobu tumbled across the sky, an armoured dragon zoomed straight at him, blasting fire from its huge mouth!

"Hold it there, human!" bellowed a voice. A Dragonoid warrior towered above him – his gun pointing right at Shobu's head!

"I don't know what you're doing out here alone," snarled the creature. "But you'll make an interesting trophy!"

Suddenly a massive explosion thundered above his head! A Rothus Blast Centurion was powering up the hillside towards them, its shoulder guns smoking!

"A Rothus coming to my rescue?!" cried Shobu. But this was no time for an explanation! As the Rothus shelled the hillside, Shobu dived for cover.

"Yaaahhh!" Shobu sat bolt upright in bed, panting and amazed. "Whoa! Where was I?"
He reached out and picked up his Duel Master cards.

"Was I inside the Duel Masters cards? In that other realm that Mr Knight talked about? But... that's nuts!"

Outside Shobu's house, Knight was sitting quietly in his car, looking serious.
"It's almost time," he muttered to himself. "The boy's potential is limitless." A jagged fork of lightning split the dark sky as Knight drove away. "I only hope I can prepare him – before the others destroy him!"

Shobu was in the gaming shop as soon as it opened, searching for information. His friends Rekuta and Kintaro were there too, buying new card packs and wondering what Shobu was doing.

"What'cha looking for, Shobu?" asked Kintaro curiously. "Strategies? New moves? Enemy weaknesses?"

"Mmm." murmured Shobu. "Nothing!" he added crossly, as he shoved another manual back on the shelf.

"Is he still at it?" asked Rekuta. "He doesn't need manuals. He actually is a Duel Master!"

"I know enough…" sighed Shobu as they left the shop and sat on the kerb outside. "Enough to know that I don't really know anything. I thought Duel Masters was just a game. But it may be much bigger than that. Winning is only part of it – and not the most important part!"

"Sounds like loser talk to me!" frowned Rekuta. But before Shobu could reply, someone stood in front of him. Shobu looked up.

"Hello Kokujo," he groaned.

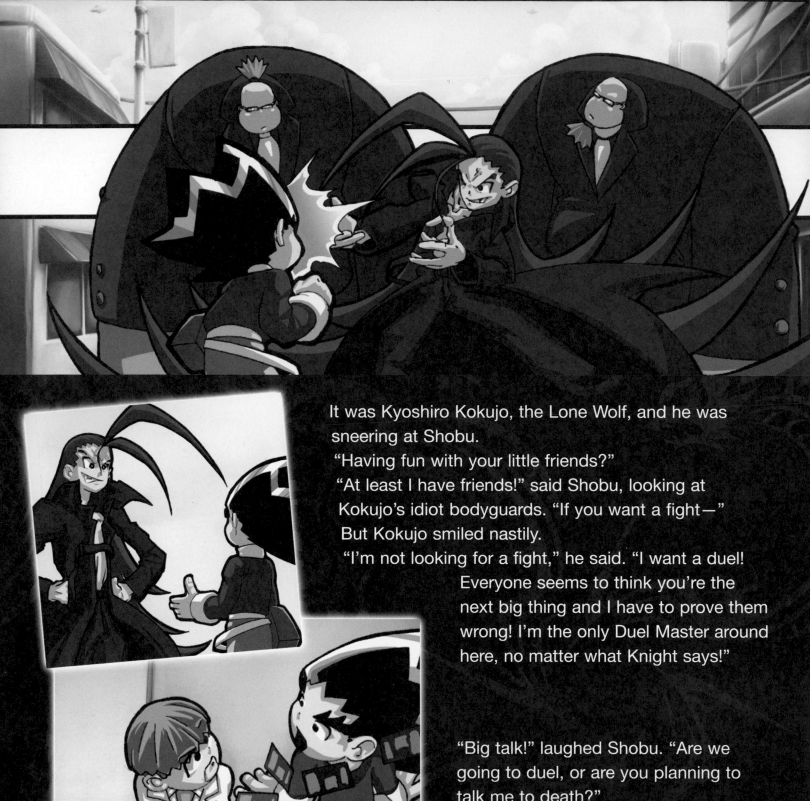

It was Kyoshiro Kokujo, the Lone Wolf, and he was sneering at Shobu.

"Having fun with your little friends?"

"At least I have friends!" said Shobu, looking at Kokujo's idiot bodyguards. "If you want a fight—"
But Kokujo smiled nastily.

"I'm not looking for a fight," he said. "I want a duel! Everyone seems to think you're the next big thing and I have to prove them wrong! I'm the only Duel Master around here, no matter what Knight says!"

"Big talk!" laughed Shobu. "Are we going to duel, or are you planning to talk me to death?"

"Behind the school this afternoon at two," said Kokujo as he walked away. "Be there!"

"Are you really going to take on the Lone Wolf?" gasped Rekuta. Shobu smiled a secretive little smile.

"Why not? I have nothing to prove and he has everything to lose! I like the odds!"

Meanwhile in the Darkness civilisation, General Dark Fried was pacing the floor and calling on her master.

"Lord Stygian!" she cried. "Hear your servant! Grant me your power in this time of war!"

A shimmering field of black energy turned into Lord Stygian, the dark power of the civilisation.

"I am here, General Fried!" he hissed. "I am the living darkness! You want what I want – the total domination of this world and the next?"

"Yes," whispered the general.

"We have a stranger here," continued Lord Stygian. "He is not of this world! There is a greater realm beyond ours, and I will own it! Rally your armies!"

"As you command, dark lord!" cried General Fried. In the Nature Civilisation, the stranger was looking around at the massive trees.

"I am as lost here as everywhere I've travelled," he said, sadly. Suddenly there was a terrifying sound behind him!

Shobu, Rekatu and Kintaro arrived at the duelling area behind the school. Kokujo was already there. Sayuki and Mimi rushed up to them.
"Is it true that you and Kokujo are going to duel?" asked Sayuki. "Is that a good idea?" "Be careful," warned Mimi. "He's ruthless and he plays for Darkness!"

"I play a Fire deck, Mimi, and fire chases darkness every time!" Shobu smiled confidently and walked towards his rival. "Let's get this duel going!" sneered Kokujo. They took their places at the playing table and placed their decks in position. It was Shobu to start and he lifted a card from his deck. A faint crackle of energy danced across his fingers and he stared at his card in surprise. "Huh?"

The crackling energy was dancing in his eyes!
"What's wrong with Shobu?" cried Kintaro.
"He looks so strange!" gasped Mimi.
Shobu was frozen still, his eyes blazing with energy and his whole body glowing with a strange light!

The robed stranger stared as a giant thundered past him. Suddenly Gigaron flew out of a huge dark cloud at the giant, which roared in fury! More terrifying beasts leaped out of the dark cloud and charged at the giant. Then a swarm of Deathblade Beetles swarmed over the hill and the creatures met in a frenzied battle! The robed man hid behind a tree. "It's like the card game come to life!" he exclaimed.

Suddenly the giant pulled the tree out of the ground and lifted it like a huge club.

The stranger lost his grip and plummeted to the ground, landing heavily in the middle of the battle! As he tried to move, the giant above him lost its balance and began to fall!

Meanwhile Shobu was still frozen in place, glowing with blazing energy!

"What kind of stupid trick is this?" yelled Kokujo. "Knock it off!"

"I don't think he can!" said Rekuta, looking very worried. "I don't think he even knows what's going on!"

"No one knows what's going on!" squeaked Mimi.

"This is not how you duel!" roared Kokujo.

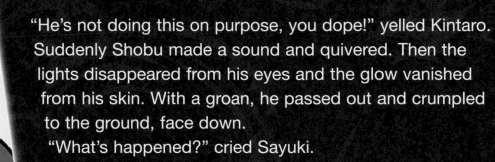

"He's not doing this on purpose, you dope!" yelled Kintaro. Suddenly Shobu made a sound and quivered. Then the lights disappeared from his eyes and the glow vanished from his skin. With a groan, he passed out and crumpled to the ground, face down.

"What's happened?" cried Sayuki.

"Someone call 999!" yelled Kintaro. What was the matter with Shobu?

WHEN WORLDS COLLIDE

TELL HIM TO *CUT IT OUT!*

GET IT THROUGH YOUR HEAD, KOKUJO, HE'S NOT *DOING* ANYTHING ON PURPOSE.

POOR GUY...

THAT WEIRD LIGHT...?

YOU SHUT UP, KYOSHIRO KOKUJO! OUR FRIEND IS IN *TROUBLE!*

ONE MINUTE SHOBU KIRIFUDA WAS PREPARING FOR A CARD DUEL, THE NEXT HE WAS FLAT ON THE GROUND, BLAZING LIKE A PARTY LANTERN.

LOOK AT HIS EYES, IT'S LIKE HE'S SEEING SOMETHING *TERRIBLE!*

THINGS DON'T GET MUCH STRANGER THAN THAT...

...OR DO THEY?

SHOBU'S EYES HAVE TRULY OPENED FOR THE VERY FIRST TIME.

NOW HE SEES INTO A HIDDEN AND TERRIBLE REALM WHERE CREATURES ROAM AND CLASH.

GRAUUUURRRR!!

WHERE A STRANGELY FAMILIAR BEING SEEMS ON THE BRINK OF MEETING HIS FATE IN THIS HARSH LANDSCAPE.

WHOA!

RELAX, IT'S JUST *TELEPORTATION*!

ZHWIIIIP

WHA... HRRRM...?!

HEY, WHAT'S GOING ON?

ARE WE GOING TO *DUEL* OR WHAT?

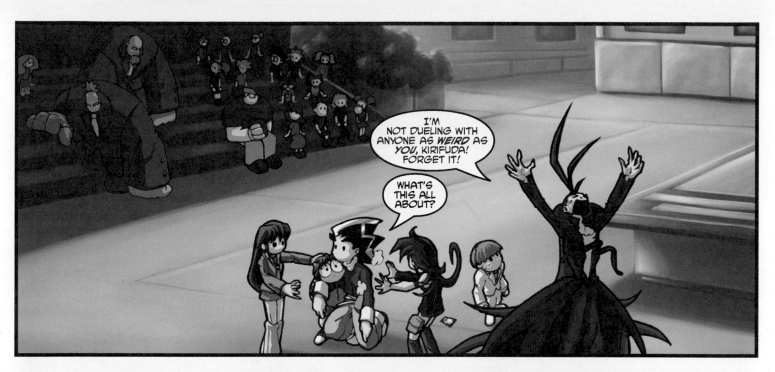

MOM, I'M *OKAY*, REALLY.

SAYUKI CALLED ME, SHE *TOLD* ME EVERYTHING.

DIDN'T SOUND *OKAY* TO ME.

I'M SORRY, SHOBU, I THOUGHT...

YOU DID THE *RIGHT THING*, SAYUKI.

YOU'RE LUCKY TO HAVE SUCH CARING FRIENDS, SHOBU.

I DO, MY FRIENDS ARE THE BEST. THEY'LL PROBABLY EVEN FORGET HOW MUCH YOU'RE EMBARRASSING ME NOW.

SHOBU, HONEY, YOU KNOW I WORRY ABOUT YOU. WITH YOUR FATHER *MISSING*...

...YOU'RE *ALL* I HAVE.

I'M SORRY, MOM. I DIDN'T MEAN TO SCARE YOU.

IT'S OKAY, SHOBU, I KNOW.

BUT I'M AFRAID I'M GOING TO HAVE TO TAKE THOSE *CARDS* FOR NOW.

HUH? WHY?!

BUT MOM... THEY'RE...

OH, ALRIGHT.

HONEY, IF THOSE IMAGES AND IDEAS ARE UPSETTING YOU THIS MUCH, YOU NEED TO TAKE A *BREAK*.

IT'S FOR YOUR OWN GOOD.

YOU AREN'T GOING TO...THROW THEM AWAY, ARE YOU?

NO, DEAR, I'LL JUST KEEP THEM FOR A WHILE.

IF YOUR FATHER WERE HERE, HE'D AGREE...

FOR AS LONG AS ANYONE CAN RECALL, OUR ONLY ENEMIES WERE OUR NEIGHBORS, THE *DRAGONOIDS!*

NOW, WE FACE ENEMIES FROM ALL THE CIVILIZATIONS AS WELL!

THE BARRIERS BETWEEN US ARE *SUNDERED!*

A DARK *POWER* IS PUSHING US ALL TO *WAR!* A WAR TO RIP OUR WORLD APART!

AND NOW, A STRANGER FROM THE *OUTER WORLD* HAS BEEN DRAWN TO US!

WHAT DOES IT ALL *MEAN?!*

I WISH I COULD TELL YOU HOW I CAME TO BE HERE.

WHILE I WAS, IN A WAY, AWARE OF THIS REALM, I CONFESS THAT I NEVER SUSPECTED THAT IT WAS *REAL*.

YOU KNOW BETTER *NOW*, EH--?

I DO, YES.

YOU KNEW OF US, BUT DIDN'T THINK US REAL?

IT'S NOT EASY TO EXPLAIN. OUR WORLDS SEEM TO BE LINKED BY THE PLAYING OF A...WELL, A *GAME*.

A GAME?! RIDICULOUS!

DO WE LOOK AS IF WE'RE *PLAYING* HERE?!

WAIT. I HAVE HEARD OF THIS BEFORE.

THERE IS OLD LORE THAT SAYS THE BRIDGE BETWEEN WORLDS HANGS ON *CHILD'S PLAY*.

IT IS ALSO SAID THAT THE GODS THEMSELVES DECIDE THE FATES OF GALAXIES BY THE THROWING OF LOTS.

PERHAPS THEY ALSO PLAY *CARDS*.

SOME *GREAT POWER* HAS CREATED THESE CARDS AT ANY RATE. OUR WORLDS HAVE BEEN *LINKED* THROUGH THE GAME... INTENTIONALLY.

I BELIEVE OUR TWO HOMES FACE THE SAME IMMANENT THREAT!

THEN YOUR COMING TO US IS THE WORK OF THE GODS. WELCOME, I AM DRAKKEN.

THIS IS MY WIFE, MORRA. THE HAIRLESS ONE IS GRYFF.

I AM KADIN.

AND I AM LOKIS. HOW ARE YOU CALLED, STRANGER?

EXCUSE ME, I'VE BEEN RUDE...

...I'M *SHORI KIRIFUDA*, PLEASED TO MEET YOU ALL.

53

WHAT WE HAVE, *YOU* HAVE, SHORI KIRIFUDA.

LET US NOW SPEAK OF REBELLION, MY FRIENDS...

HAVE YOU WAYS TO FIGHT THIS UNKNOWN FORCE WHICH SPREADS CONFLICT?

THERE IS A WARRIOR RACE FROM THE DARKNESS CIVILIZATION KNOWN TO *SERVE* IT! *THEY* CAN BE FOUGHT!

AND IF WE CAN ALERT THE OTHER RACES OF THIS *MANIPULATION*, WE CAN *UNITE* AGAINST THIS EVIL!

WE MIGHT EVEN ENLIST THE AID OF THOSE WHO DWELL IN THE *LIGHT*.

IF I'M RIGHT, EARTH IS IN JUST AS MUCH DANGER. IF ONLY THERE WAS SOME WAY TO GET THE WORD TO THEM TOO...

THERE MIGHT BE A WAY, SHORI KIRIFUDA!

THERE IS *ONE* WHO MIGHT JUST BE ABLE TO TRAVEL WHERE NO ONE ELSE CAN--!

I MAKE NO EXCUSES. MY ACTIONS ARE MY VOICE. I HAVE NO ENEMIES. MY OPPONENT IS MY TEACHER.

I NEED NO DECEITFUL TRICKS. MY CHARACTER IS MY SWORD. I THINK NOT OF DEFEAT. MY COURAGE IS MY SECRET WEAPON.

I KNOW NOT OF DEFEAT. MY EXPERIENCE BECOMES MY STRENGTH.

SOON IT WILL BE SHOBU KIRIFUDA'S TURN TO LEARN THE *KAIJUDO CODE.*

HOPEFULLY, IT ALSO BRINGS STRENGTH AND COURAGE TO THE BOY'S FATHER--*WHEREVER* HE IS.

I SENSE THAT WE WILL SOON *KNOW* WHERE SHORI HAS GONE.

BUT THAT *REUNION* MAY WELL BE FURTHER DELAYED BY *COMING CONFLICT.* WE MUST BE READY.

READY FOR *ANYTHING.*

KNOCK KNOCK KNOCK

MR. KNIGHT?!

YES...?

AH, IT IS *YOU*. WELCOME.

COME IN, MS. TASOGARE. HOW MAY I BE OF SERVICE--?

DROP THE ACT, KNIGHT, WE HAVE *TROUBLE*.

ALRIGHT, WHAT'S GOING ON, MIMI?

SHOBU *PASSED OUT* AND STARTED *GLOWING* THIS AFTERNOON, FOR ONE THING.

I SEE. THAT *IS* UNEXPECTED, IF NOT OVERLY ALARMING.

FOR *YOU*, MAYBE NOT. IT SCARED THE HECK OUT OF ME!

THAT'S NOT ALL. HIS MOTHER TOOK AWAY HIS CARD DECK!

ALL RIGHT, *THAT* IS MORE ALARMING.

THAT COULD LEAVE HIM *DEFENSELESS.*

SO, YOU'LL *FIX* IT?

IT MAY NOT BE SO EASY. MAI IS JUST TRYING TO PROTECT HER SON.

I THINK SHE ALSO FEARS THE CARDS ARE BEHIND HER HUSBAND'S *DISAPPEARANCE.*

I'LL DO WHAT I CAN. THANK YOU FOR COMING.

IN THE MEANTIME, WE MUST ALL BE VIGILANT.